BEHAVIOR MANAGEMENT
Strategies and Techniques

Susan K. Peterson
Henry A. Tenenbaum

UNIVERSITY
PRESS OF
AMERICA

LANHAM • NEW YORK • LONDON

Copyright © 1986 by

University Press of America,® Inc.

4720 Boston Way
Lanham, MD 20706

3 Henrietta Street
London WC2E 8LU England

Library of Congress Cataloging in Publication Data

Peterson, Susan K., 1956-
  Behavior management.

  Bibliography: p.
  1. Classroom management.   2. School children—
Discipline.   3. Behavior modification.   I. Tenenbaum,
Henry A.   II. Title.
LB3013.P44   1986   371.1'024   86-9113
ISBN 0-8191-5361-3 (alk. paper)
ISBN 0-8191-5362-1 (pbk. : alk. paper)

All University Press of America books are produced on acid-free
paper which exceeds the minimum standards set by the National
Historical Publications and Records Commission.

To children whose behaviors need managing

and to their teachers.

ACKNOWLEDGMENTS

It is appropriate to acknowledge the assistance of Ron Burnett, Cecil Mercer, Sarah Tenenbaum, and Bill Wolking. Their suggestions and support helped bring this task to completion. A special thanks to Terry Findley for her meticulous and invaluable help in preparing the manuscript. Finally, we would like to thank our parents for providing our initial experiences with behavior management.

TABLE OF CONTENTS

PREFACE

Behavior management in the classroom continues to be a major concern to teachers, administrators and parents. Teachers commonly express uncertainties regarding how to achieve "good discipline" in their classrooms. Discipline, in fact, is one of the most persistent problems reported in surveys of teachers.

Many recommendations for improving student behaviors have been reported in the literature, and the importance of classroom management is extensively recognized. Yet, it is not uncommon to find conflicting ideas and vague rules regarding classroom management. To add to this problem, teachers often feel their college or university training did not adequately prepare them for the realities of teaching.

Systematic research on behavior management has increased in recent years. Therefore, more is known about effective classroom management. The Multidisciplinary Diagnostic and Training Program, housed at the University of Florida, has experimented with a variety of behavioral interventions--these and others are reported in this text. The purpose is to identify a variety of general strategies and specific techniques that teachers may implement to improve student performance and behavior.

INTRODUCTION

Behavior Management: Strategies and Techniques presents general strategies for encouraging appropriate student behaviors. Included among these are providing structure through scheduling, creating a positive environment, being consistent, and planning for instruction. Part I of the text presents specific management techniques that may be helpful when general strategies are not enough to maintain desirable student behavior. Fourteen techniques are included. Possible target behaviors, an overall description of the techniques, steps for implementation, and supportive research are included for each. Part II of the text presents an overview of reinforcement, punishment, and behavior measurement. Teacher knowledge in these areas will promote a positive environment for academic and behavioral learning.

PART I

GENERAL STRATEGIES

Successful classroom management should involve the prevention of behavioral problems before they have a chance to manifest themselves (Good & Brophy, 1978; Doyle, 1980). Several general strategies have been developed to assist in this aspect of classroom management.

Provide Structure through Scheduling

Structure involves the establishment of clear daily goals with procedures that are understood by both the teacher and student. The instructional activities should relate to the identified goals. Scheduling is vital for accomplishing goals in an organized fashion. Most students with behavior problems need the organization and routine provided with a systematic daily schedule. Students who have a daily schedule to follow are better equipped to pace their own work in an efficient manner (Evertson, Emmer, Clements, Sanford, & Worsham, 1984). Moreover, these students know what behaviors are expected (Gallagher, 1979; Orelove, 1982).

To devise a daily schedule the teacher must analyze daily events, her instructional goals, and the amount of time she has available for direct contact with the students. District guidelines must be examined regarding the amount of time that should be allotted for different subjects. Music and art may need to be offered for one hour each week. In each case, the teacher must arrange her daily schedule around these predetermined activities.

Mercer & Mercer (1985) suggest beginning each day with opening activities and ending the day with closing activities. Opening activities involve taking attendance, collecting lunch money, saluting the flag, recognizing special days, discussing the daily schedule, and discussing current events. This time may also be used for short affective educational exercises or for show and tell. Closing activities are used for summerizing the day, putting away supplies, and determining what to take home.

Many teachers find students more alert in the morning than in the afternoon. Therefore, they find it helpful to plan the intensive academic instruction in the morning. These instructional activities are not always teacher directed. They may also include such things as learning centers, independent seatwork, or peer teaching. Large group-oriented lessons are then planned for the afternoon. These could include art, physical education, storytime, and chorus. Teachers will most likely need to experiment with schedules to determine which works best in their situation.

Create a Positive Environment

Providing a positive classroom environment is essential. Students need to feel accepted and respected. They need to experience success. Verbal praise for appropriate behaviors is a powerful strategy and should be provided throughout the school day (Broden, Bruce, Mitchell, Carter, & Hall, 1970; Luiselli & Downing, 1980). Attention given to the student should be contingent upon acceptable behavior or on close approximations of expected behavior (i.e. "I like the way Jennifer is working quietly" or "I like the way Matthew is getting ready to begin his assignment"). Such comments encourage students to maintain on-task behaviors, build self-confidence, and promote positive interactions in the class.

Be Consistent

The need for consistency is stressed throughout the behavior management literature. Yet, its meaning is not always clear. For application in the classroom, consistency means "retaining the same expectations for appropriate behavior in an activity at all times and for all students" (Evertson, Emmer, Clements, Sanford, & Worsham, 1984, p. 99). Establishing consistency initially will prevent many future problems. This can be accomplished by using positive classroom rules that are appropriate and easily understood. The teacher must feel strongly enough about the rules to enforce them, or it becomes difficult to maintain consistency. Some teachers feel they can be more consistent if they establish a task-oriented or business-like classroom. According to Rosenshine and Furst (1973) there is a direct correlation between task-oriented classrooms and student achievement.

Plan for Instruction

A comprehensive plan for instruction is needed to promote a meaningful learning environment. This plan should consider physical space, instructional arrangements, educational materials, and classroom procedures.

A classroom's physical arrangement influences the instructional program and student attitudes. An effective use of physical space involves dividing the classroom into distinct areas equipped for specific activities (Brophy, 1983). Learning centers provide a means for such organization. They can include instructional games, practice sheets, and other activities that provide instruction on specific skill areas.

When organizing classroom space, provisions should be made for small-group and large-group instruction. Space for storing materials must be planned so that it is convenient and easy to manage. Well organized space encourages smooth transitions between activities, provides reasonable traffic patterns, and contributes to positive classroom interactions.

Mercer & Mercer (1985) identify five basic instructional arrangements available to teachers. These include large group with teacher,

2

small group with teacher, one student with teacher, peer teaching, and material with students. Which arrangement the teacher selects at any given point should be dependent upon the established goals. It is suggested that teachers use varying instructional arrangements to promote interest and variety when meeting the needs of their children.

Educational material selection is crucial for planning learning activities. Materials affect the content, quality, and efficiency of an instructional program (Mercer & Mercer, 1985). According to Wilson (1978) 75-99% of each student's instructional time is planned around educational materials. This clearly indicates the need for careful selection and appropriate management of materials. Three options are available to teachers who are choosing materials for their classroom. They may adopt a commercial material and use it as designed, adapt a commercial material to fit the instructional needs of a particular student, or make their own materials (Archer & Edgar, 1976). In every case, however, the materials selected should be motivating and on the student's instructional level.

A final element involved in planning for instruction requires the establishment of classroom procedures. These procedures vary with different classrooms. However, effectively managed classrooms do not attempt to operate without them. Procedures should be established for entering and leaving the room, turning in materials, participating in lessons, and checking student work. Procedures for room use, expected behaviors of students, distributing materials, and fire drills are also helpful (Evertson, et al., 1984).

Implementation of effective classroom strategies will increase the likelihood that students will exhibit appropriate behaviors and decrease the number of discipline problems. With some students additional strategies will be needed to maintain a classroom environment conducive to learning.

Long and Newman (1971) developed 12 strategies for managing surface behaviors observed in the classroom. These strategies are designed to prevent the buildup of problem behaviors. They include the following:

1.   Planned ignoring--Many inappropriate behaviors will decrease when they are ignored. Students are given attention for appropriate behavior.

2.   Proximity control--Some disruptive behaviors can be prevented by the close physical presence of the teacher. Teacher mobility in the classroom is a viable tool in behavior management.

3.   Signal interference—These are cues from the teacher that alert students to discontinue a particular behavior (i.e. clearing throat, staring).

3

4. Interest boosting--Typically, behaviors of children may be managed more effectively if the teacher has established rapport with the students. One way to do this is to initiate conversation regarding the students' interests. A variation of this technique is for the teacher to display an interest in the student's work itself.

5. Tension decontamination through humor--A humorous remark or joke can release tension during an emotional situation.

6. Hurdle lessons--The teacher may be able to reduce student frustration by providing special assistance with difficult academic tasks.

7. Restructuring the classroom program--This technique involves a change in plans, format, task or location based on a need to reduce tension in the classroom.

8. Support from routine--Having an established routine or daily schedule can promote appropriate classroom behavior and thus minimize misbehavior.

9. Direct appeal to value areas--The teacher can appeal to the student's personal values to encourage appropriate behavior.

10. Removing seductive objects--Items which distract the student may be removed from the work area.

11. Antiseptic bounce--The teacher may send the student out of the room to deliver a message, borrow something from another teacher, or get a drink of water. This is a nonpunitive action that allows the student to save face and possibly avoid a serious flare-up.

12. Physical restraint--When a student exhibits aggressive behavior that may result in physical injury to himself or others, it may be necessary to restrain the student.

Using these general management strategies and surface management strategies will prevent many problem behaviors in the classroom.

SPECIFIC TECHNIQUES

Using general management strategies alone will not always meet all the needs of all students. Occasionally additional management systems are needed to promote and monitor appropriate behavior for an entire class or for certain individuals within the class. This is particularly true when serving special education students in self-contained settings, resource rooms, or in mainstreamed regular classroom environments. Current research indicates that many techniques in this text are successful for improving student behavior; however, every technique will not be effective with all children. Instead the intent is to provide a repertoire of ideas for the reader. Furthermore, modifications of these interventions may be necessary for implementation in a particular setting. Teachers are encouraged to examine individual student needs, specific classroom environment, and their own personal teaching style. Consideration of such factors assists in selecting the intervention and increases the possibility of successful behavior management.

A number of intervention techniques are presented that may be used in regular or special educational settings. Of course, any strategy must be well-planned and tried several times before judgment of its effectiveness can be made. The target behaviors listed for each intervention are not all inclusive. The included interventions are effective with a multitude of behaviors (see Appendix).

5

Beat the Clock

Target Behaviors

COMPLIANCE
> Completing work within a designated amount of time
> Staying on task

Description

This intervention is designed to motivate those students who typically work much slower than they should. These students are able to perform the assignment, but do so at a much slower pace than is expected based on their ability level. This technique adheres to the premise that time devices can be helpful in managing student behavior (Paine, Radicchi, Rosellini, Deutchman, & Dorch, 1983). A kitchen timer is convenient to use as it provides audible and visual feedback to the student.

Implementation

These steps are suggested for implementing this intervention.

1. Identify the assignment to be completed.

2. Identify the amount of time the student will be given to complete the assignment.

3. Tell the student his goal is to "beat the clock." In other words, complete the assignment before the timer bell rings.

4. Instruct the student to raise his hand as soon as he finishes the work.

5. If the student completes the assignment and raises his hand before the timer rings, he may be rewarded with a sticker, a star, or a certificate. For many students, however, beating the clock is reward enough when paired with verbal praise.

6. This system may be extended to include both time and accuracy. This is especially helpful with those children who increase their speed but decrease accuracy in the process.

Research

This intervention has been successfully implemented in the Multi-disciplinary Diagnostic and Training Program classroom located at the University of Florida. This technique has been effective with all elementary grade levels and with learning disabled, emotionally handi-capped, educably mentally handicapped, and regular education students who have behavioral or learning problems (Peterson, 1985). Rainwater and Ayllon (1976) used a timing procedure to increase the reading and math performance of first grade students. In this study, simply telling the students they were being timed increased their work rates. The authors suggest, however, that to maintain this effect some feedback or timing device is needed.

Behavioral Self-control (BSC)

Target Behaviors

ACADEMIC IMPROVEMENT
　　Increasing accuracy of work
　　Increasing number of completed assignments

AFFECTIVE
　　Keeping hands in right place

AGGRESSION
　　Maintaining non-aggressive behavior

COMPLIANCE
　　Staying on task
　　Staying in seat
　　Working quietly
　　Raising hand

Description

Behavioral Self-Control gives students the opportunity to manage their own behavior with the teacher and other supporting adults, teaches students to accept responsibility for their own behavior and enhances the maintenance and generalization of behavior modification programs (Workman, 1982).

The Behavioral Self-Control technique has three basic components including self-assessment, self-monitoring, and self-reinforcement. Self-assessment refers to students systematically examining and evaluating their own behavior. For example, students may rate their on-task behavior on a scale from one to five. Self-monitoring is a procedure whereby students systematically monitor and record their performance on particular behaviors. This may involve keeping track of how often they engage in some activity. Self-reinforcement refers to students giving themselves reinforcers for appropriate behavior. It is based on the principle of positive reinforcement (Workman, 1982).

Implementation

The following steps have been suggested for implementing a BSC Self-Assessment program (Workman, 1982).

1. Identify the target behavior.
2. Devise a rating system.
3. Decide on the rating system interval.
4. Design a student-rating form and scoring system that students can maintain.
5. Explain the system to the student and begin.

The following are suggested steps for implementing a self-monitoring procedure in the classroom.

1. Identify the target behaviors.
2. Design the students' recording sheets.
3. Give the sheets to the students.
4. Tell the students exactly what behavior to record and that they should try to improve.
5. Have the students record and chart their behavior.

The following steps are suggested for implementing a self-reinforcement system.

1. Identify target behaviors.
2. Determine the time interval.
3. Determine recording method students will use.
4. Establish a method to signal students to monitor and record the target behavior (i.e. kitchen timer, verbally announce).
5. Have students monitor and record the target behavior for two to three days.
6. Select back-up reinforcers that could be used to motivate students.
7. Determine the number of intervals in which most students are engaged in the target behavior. This should be done several days after the initial recording begins.
8. The criterion for reinforcement should be set just above the number of intervals during which most students engage in the target behavior. A good rule of thumb is a 20% to 25% increase over the number of intervals in step 7.
9. Explain your system to the students in detail.
10. Begin the system.
11. If needed, implement a procedure to increase the accuracy of the students' recording.
12. Increase the criterion slightly when most students are consistently reaching the criterion for one or two weeks.
13. To ensure that the reinforcers remain desirable, periodically check student preferences. Change the reinforcement menu if needed.

For more details regarding the implementation of behavioral self-control techniques refer to Teaching Behavioral Self-Control to Students by Edward A. Workman.

Research

The purpose of teaching self-control skills to students is to provide them with the ability to give themselves feedback on their own behavior. BSC teaches students to take responsibility for their own actions. BSC has been successfully used to increase on-task behaviors (Workman & Hector, 1978). BSC techniques have also been used to decrease disruptive behaviors and thus improve students' school performance (Workman & Hector, 1978). Additional research has investigated the effects of the three basic components which comprise BSC (Blackwood, 1970; Kaufman & O'Leary, 1972; Bornstein & Quevillon, 1976; Piersal & Kratochwill, 1979; Moletzky, 1974; Glynn, et al., 1973; Humphrey & Karoly, 1978; Bolstad & Johnson, 1972). Each demonstrates BSC's effectiveness in terms of increasing on-task behavior, reducing disruptive behavior, or increasing academic achievement.

BSC has been used in the Multidisciplinary Diagnostic classroom at the University of Florida to reduce negative statements and increase positive statements (Peterson, 1984). Students use wrist counters to record negative statements. When these statements decrease to criterion, the students begin counting positive statements.

Cognitive Modeling

Target Behaviors

ACADEMIC IMPROVEMENT
  Increasing academic skills
AFFECTIVE
  Improving problem solving abilities
  Improving self-control skills
AGGRESSION
  Maintaining nonaggressive behaviors
COMPLIANCE
  Decreasing talk-out behavior

Description

Cognitive modeling involves the manipulation of antecedents (before response of the child) and consequences (after response of the child) to change overt and covert behavior. This intervention involves modeling and verbal rehearsal, such as verbal mediation, self-instruction, or problem-solving procedures. Students using cognitive modeling imitate and rehearse target behaviors aloud, in a whisper, and finally silently. This method is often used to develop self-control in students (Olson, 1982).

Implementation

Olson (1982) suggests the following steps for implementing cognitive modeling.

1. Cue the student to attend to both the physical and verbal actions of the model.
2. Choose one of the following verbal recitation procedures.
   a. The model describes the model's feelings as the task is completed.
   b. The model describes the step-by-step procedures necessary to complete the task.
   c. The model describes the problem-solving strategies used.
3. Instruct the students to copy the model's statements aloud as they complete the task.
4. Have the students rehearse the model's verbalization while thinking aloud without the teacher's help.
5. Have the students whisper the self-verbalizations as they complete the task.
6. Instruct the students to perform the verbalizations and the task using private speech.
7. Have the students evaluate how well they copied the verbal and physical actions of the model.
8. Socially praise or reinforce the students throughout the process.

Research

Cognitive modeling is a relatively new and exciting strategy. It merges the management of inner thought and overt behavior. Camp and Bash (1978) successfully used cognitive modeling with aggressive children. In their procedure the model defined the problem, verbally listed the possible solutions, mentioned some appropriate general behaviors, and evaluated. Eaton and Hansen (1978) used a mediating written model to decrease talking-out behavior. They report the number of talk-outs decreased significantly.

Lochman, Burch, Curry, and Lampron (1984) successfully implemented cognitive-behavioral techniques to 76 aggressive boys. One month follow-up testing indicated the boys had reduced their disruptive and aggressive behavior in the classroom, had decreased their aggression at home, and displayed a tendency for improved perceptions of self-esteem.

Contracting

Target Behaviors

ACADEMIC IMPROVEMENT
  Improving skills/grades
  Increasing accuracy of work
AFFECTIVE
  Participating in group
AGGRESSION
  Maintaining nonaggressive behavior
COMPLIANCE
  Being on time to class
  Completing academic tasks
  Sitting properly
  Staying in seat
  Walking while in classroom

Description

Contracting is easy to implement and highly adaptable to individual differences among student interests, maturity, and aptitude. This intervention helps students to become self-sufficient and responsible learners.

The student and teacher select a mutually agreeable activity and write it in the form of a contract. These contracts make a student's behavior contingent on a reward which the teacher will deliver. This intervention adheres to principles such as "Eat all your supper, then you may have dessert" or "Finish your work, then you may play."

One advantage of contracting systems is their flexibility in terms of structuring to permit differing degrees of teacher control versus student autonomy. At one end of the continuum the student requirements may be very detailed and specific. At the other end, they may only indicate the type of final outcome desired (i.e. develop a display on measurement for the math contest). Thus the student is given the freedom to make numerous decisions and still meet the requirements of the contract. A decision regarding how much structure to provide in the written contract should be made dependent upon the goals of instruction and the self-control level of the student (Murphy & Ross, 1983).

It is also possible to use contracting with an entire class. Group contracts involve having the whole class agree to maintain certain behaviors or perform a specified task by a specific date. The teacher agrees to reward the students who fulfill the contractual agreement (Mercer & Mercer, 1985).

Implementation

The following steps have been suggested for developing a contingency contract (Stephens, 1977).

1. The specific behavior required of the student is outlined.
2. The reinforcement for which the student will work is identified. This reinforcement is only administered when the student performs the specific behaviors.
3. The terms of the contract are determined. This includes the amount or type of behavior required, the amount or type of reward, and any existing time constraints.
4. The teacher evaluates student performance and then rewards when the conditions of the contract have been met.

Typically a short orientation process occurs when contracting is first introduced to a class or student. The purposes and procedures of contracting are explained to the student. The students are given an opportunity to ask questions to clarify their understanding. It is critical that students understand how a contract works and what their role in the process involves.

The contract itself (see Figures 1 and 2) should state the desired or target behavior, the criterion for performance, and the beginning and ending dates. The student and teacher should sign the contract. It may also be helpful to include the signature of a witness.

Research

Contracting has been a popular intervention for addressing behavioral problems of learning disabled students for a long time (Mahoney & Thoresen, 1974). Lovitt's (1973) work on contingency management demonstrates that contracting has great potential for application to academic concerns as well. There is further evidence that behavior disordered children can set their own contingencies and actually exceed their previous performance while under teacher imposed contingencies (Lovitt, 1973).

Figure 1

Sample of Teacher-Child Contract Form

CONTRACT

Name _David McLaughlin_ Date _9/20_

If _David completes his math,_

reading, and language arts

seatwork

_____ by _11:30 a.m._

Then _he may have 15 minutes_

of computer time

Figure 2

Sample of Teacher-Child Contract Form

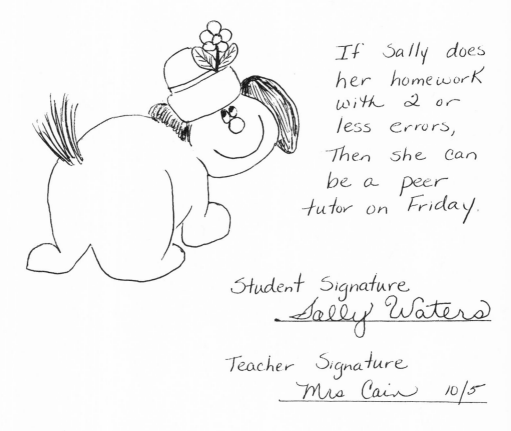

Sally's Contract

If Sally does
her homework
with 2 or
less errors,
Then she can
be a peer
tutor on Friday.

Student Signature
Sally Waters

Teacher Signature
Mrs Cain 10/5

The Good Behavior Game

Target Behaviors

AFFECTIVE
  Keeping hands in the right place
AGGRESSION
  Maintaining nonaggressive behavior
COMPLIANCE
  Raising hand
  Staying in seat
  Working quietly

Description

The Good Behavior Game is a group management game which incorporates reinforcement, stimulus control, punishment, and differential reinforcement of other behaviors. It was devised to help teachers who have seriously disruptive students in their classrooms. If the general atmosphere is chaotic with numerous children displaying inappropriate behaviors, then this intervention may be helpful. This type of group contingency offers several advantages. It is easy to implement and does not require the teacher to attend to every individual student with reinforcement. Moreover, students seem to enjoy the game (Azaroff & Mayer, 1977).

Implementation

Lovitt (1984) and Barrish, Saunders, and Wolf (1969) established the following steps for implementing the Good Behavior Game.

1. Tell the class that the inappropriate behaviors will no longer be tolerated. Moreover, each incident will be counted.
2. Identify and define the target behaviors.
3. Tell the student that every time someone fails to exhibit the target behaviors, a mark will be written by his name.
4. Divide the class into two teams and have them sit on opposite sides of the room.
5. At the end of the designated period or at the end of the day, announce the team who had the fewest total marks by their names. This is the winning team. Both teams win if they each have fewer than five marks.
6. Reward the winning team with one of the following:
    a. Victory badges to wear
    b. Thirty minutes of free time
    c. Privilege of lining up first
    d. Stars or stickers beside their names on a winner's chart
    e. Extra recess time
7. Tell the members of the losing team they will not receive these privileges until they win the game.

17

Research

The Good Behavior Game was first implemented by Barrish, Saunders, and Wolf (1969) in a fourth grade class. The two rules used for this game were "stay in seat" and "only talk to classmates if given permission." Later, Harris and Sherman (1973) implemented the game in fifth and sixth grade classrooms to reduce throwing objects, whistling, and talking out. In both studies disruptive student behavior was significantly reduced.

Darveaux (1984) modified the Good Behavior Game to include a token reinforcement system. This intervention proved successful in reducing disruptive behavior and improving assignment completion of second grade students.

Independent Work Chart

Target Behaviors

COMPLIANCE
>Beginning work immediately after directions
>Finishing the assignment
>Staying in seat
>Staying on task
>Working quietly

Description

This intervention involves the establishment of a contingency based on the student's ability to demonstrate at least four of the five targeted behaviors for independent seatwork. A chart is made which contains the days of the week and the five target behaviors (see Figure 3). This chart is taped to the student's desk top to serve as a cue for the appropriate behaviors. The chart is only used when the student is expected to work independently without teacher directed instruction. If the student successfully exhibits four of the behaviors, he is rewarded with a sticker, star, or good worker certificate. When the student consistently demonstrates four of the behaviors, the criterion may be extended to earning the reward when all five behaviors are performed. This intervention may be used in conjunction with a more general management plan (e.g., a token economy system). When this is the case, the reward may be earning "bonus" tokens.

Implementation

Several steps are suggested for implementing this intervention.

1. Identify the target behaviors for working independently.
2. Discuss these behaviors with the student using the chart which has been taped to the desk top.
3. Instruct the student to raise his hand when he finishes the assignment.
4. Give the student instructions for the assignment and then walk away from his working area.
5. Watch for the targeted behaviors, but do not interact with the student unless he raises his hand and asks an assignment related question.
6. When the student raises his hand to signify he is finished, immediately fill in the independent work chart. Smiley faces or checkmarks may be placed under the target behaviors that were demonstrated. It is helpful to verbalize these to the student (i.e., you stayed in your seat, you worked quietly, etc.).

19

Figure 3.

Independent Work Chart Sample Form

NAME	BEGIN WORK IMMEDIATELY	STAY IN SEAT	QUIET	STAY ON TASK	FINISH WORK	TOTAL FOR DAY
MONDAY						
TUESDAY						
WEDNESDAY						
THURSDAY						
FRIDAY						

7.   If the student accomplishes the predetermined criterion (e.g. 4/5 smiley faces), he is rewarded; if not, the teacher verbalizes what he must do differently next time to earn the reward.

Research

The Independent Work Chart was designed by a classroom teacher in the Multidisciplinary Diagnostic and Training Program at the University of Florida.   It has been successful with a number of students who had problems completing independent seat work (Peterson, 1985).   This chart has been used with learning disabled students, emotionally handicapped students, educably mentally handicapped students, and regular education students who had behavioral or learning problems.

Modeling

Target Behaviors

AFFECTIVE
   Cooperating with peers
   Promoting positive relationships
   Verbalizing positively
AGGRESSION
   Maintaining nonaggressive behavior
COMPLIANCE
   Raising hand
   Walking while in classroom
   Working quietly

Description

Modeling is a technique whereby the student learns appropriate behaviors from observing and imitating others. Three types of modeling have been identified. These include modeling of peers, modeling of fictitious or idealized characters, and modeling of an important adult (Wolfgang & Glickman, 1980).

The use of peer modeling is implemented when teachers praise students who are exhibiting target behaviors so that students in close proximity will learn what behaviors result in positive consequences. This modeling process can teach new behaviors or strengthen previously learned behaviors (Mercer & Mercer, 1985). Students typically respond to the inappropriate behaviors of their schoolmates with giggles, mimics, stomps or imitations. If the peers, however, feel partially responsible for improving the inappropriate behaviors, they are better able to monitor their own reactions. Moreover, using peer models offers the teacher assistance in class management which provides additional time for other necessary services (Lovitt, 1984).

Storybook characters and T.V. characters can also be used for modeling appropriate and/or inappropriate behavior. The idea is to present individuals with whom children can identify.

The last form of modeling involves a significant adult who is important to the child. A teacher often fits this description, especially with younger students. Children often imitate adults who exhibit characteristics they would like to have (Wolfgang & Glickman, 1980).

Implementation

The following steps have been suggested for implementing modeling procedures (Mercer & Mercer, 1985).

1.   Identify the behavior.
2.   Identify the model.

22

3. Give directions to the model and the observer concerning their roles.
4. Reinforce the model for exhibiting the appropriate behavior.
5. Reinforce the observer for imitating the appropriate behavior.

Research

Mitchell and Milan (1983) found that modeling alone is insufficient to reliably produce enduring, clinically-significant changes in behavior. However, when reinforcement for imitation was included in the modeling effort, imitation increased and was maintained at high levels of performance. Thus, the modeling with reinforced imitation paradigm is effective for practical classroom purposes.

Another study specifically involving peers demonstrated the effectiveness of modeling for changing disruptive behaviors such as talk outs, out of seats, and inappropriate playing (Solomon & Wahler, 1973). Again modeling and reinforcement were used together.

Csapo's (1972) findings indicate success with peer modeling in a regular primary classroom. In this research the peer models were used during the academic part of the day only. These studies indicate applications for modeling in a variety of settings.

Peer Tutoring

Target Behaviors

ACADEMIC IMPROVEMENT
Increasing accuracy of work
Increasing skill progress
AFFECTIVE
Cooperating with peers
Decreasing shyness
Improving self-esteem
Promoting positive relationships

Description

Peer tutoring is a strategy in which one student is paired with another student who is having difficulty in a particular academic area. In addition to providing direct one-to-one instruction on academic skills, peer tutoring can also be used to improve social skills. Students who are selected to be tutors often improve their behavioral problems and their self-concept.

The teacher is responsible for determining which skills should be taught and which materials and methods should be used. The teacher should train the peer tutor in teaching and reinforcement techniques. The peer tutor assumes the teacher role, provides the instruction, provides appropriate feedback, and evaluates the tasks.

Implementation

Olson (1982) suggested the following steps for implementing peer tutoring.

1. Identify objectives for the tutoring program.
2. Identify the role of the peer tutor (i.e. academic tutor or behavioral manager).
3. Identify and match tutees to tutors.
4. Select the tutoring site.
5. Hold an orientation meeting with the tutors.
6. Schedule the tutoring sessions.
7. Train the tutors to teach or manage.
8. Design a feedback system.

Research

Cloward (1967) reports that peer tutoring is commonly practiced in regular education classes. Allen (1976) indicates that peer tutoring has a positive effect on the tutor. His study showed that the tutors improved academic difficulties or behavior difficulties and in some cases both. Shafer, Egel, and Neef (1984) discuss the effects of a peer-training strategy on the occurrence and duration of interactions between autistic students and nonautistic peer-trainers. Their results show immediate and substantial increases in positive social interactions. These increases maintained during subsequent free-play probes. Another study (Greenwood et al, 1984) compared teacher to peer-mediated instruction. The results indicate that classwide peer tutoring, compared to the teacher's procedure, produced more student academic responding and higher weekly test scores among upper elementary school children. Peer tutoring has also been used to increase social interactions betwen nonhandicapped and handicapped students. (Nietupski et al, 1983). In sum, peer tutoring has been used successfully to improve academic skills, foster self-esteem, help the shy student, help students who have difficulty with authority figures, improve race relations, and promote positive relationships and cooperation among classmates (Mercer & Mercer, 1985).

Reality Therapy

Target Behaviors

AFFECTIVE
Improving problem solving abilities
Increasing responsible behavior
Increasing socially acceptable behaviors

Description

Reality therapy is a cognitive technique that teaches children to actively change their overt behaviors. Children learn to describe and evaluate their behavior through teacher directed questioning. Students also learn to develop a plan for changing their behavior so that it is more responsible and socially acceptable. Class meetings are held whereby the students are able to express their concerns about school, home, and other areas of their life. Reality therapy is both a preventative and remedial program in that it attempts to change behavior before and after it occurs. It can be used with individuals or groups. Discipline and a warm student-teacher relationship are necessary for this technique to be effective (Olson, 1982).

Implementation

Olson (1982) suggests the following implementation steps for individual therapy.

1. Build a trusting relationship and establish rapport with the student.
2. When the student exhibits an inappropriate behavior, ask him what he is doing. If the child does not respond, describe what was seen and question the student further (i.e., I saw you tear your paper; then what did you do?). The goal is for the student to verbalize the entire situation with minimal teacher input. The child should never be asked why he behaved a certain way because this allows him to rationalize the behavior or blame it on someone else.
3. Guide the student to make a value judgment regarding his behavior.
4. Ask the student to devise a plan which lists alternative behaviors.
5. Guide the student to make a commitment to one of the alternatives.
6. Follow through to determine if the student is following the plan.
7. No excuses are accepted for failure to follow the plan. The student must face the natural consequences (i.e., failing a test, staying after school). The consequences should not be adjusted.

8. The child should be isolated if he refuses to participate in any of the steps. This should not be done in a punitive manner, but the student must have a plan or agree to participate before rejoining the class.

The following steps are suggested for implementing reality therapy in a group setting (Olson, 1982).

1. Seat the children in a circle. The teacher also sits in the circle positioning herself by different children at each meeting.
2. Glasser (1965) suggests holding one meeting a day for elementary students and twice a week for adolescents. The meeting should last from 10 to 30 minutes.
3. Select the type of meeting to be held (i.e., open-ended, educational, diagnostic, or social problem solving).
4. Introduce the topic.
5. Ask the students to respond to the problem. Students who do not want to say anything may pass.
6. The following strategies may be used in social problem-solving meetings.
   a. Direct the comments toward solving the problem.
   b. Lead the students to understand there are many solutions to a problem.
   c. Enforce the group's decision plan.

Research

Reality therapy is designed to change inner attitudes and overt behaviors of children through discipline, a warm teacher-student relationship, and questioning techniques. William Glasser (1978) has promoted the use of reality therapy and has reported its success with emotionally disturbed children.

Response Cost System

Target Behaviors

AFFECTIVE
  Verbalizing positively
AGGRESSION
  Maintaining nonaggressive behavior
COMPLIANCE
  Being on time to class

Description

A response-cost system involves the removal or withdrawal of a quantity of reinforcers, contingent upon a particular response. For example, a student may lose points or tokens or a few minutes of recess for hitting another individual in the classroom. To remove these specified amounts of a reinforcer, the student must have "some level of positive reinforcement. . .available in order to provide the opportunity for . . .withdrawing that reinforcement" (Azrin & Holz, 1966, p. 392). Those using response cost systems should know they involve aversive procedures that may evoke counter-control behaviors. Response cost has, however, been incorporated into many behavioral programs with successful results (Azaroff & Mayer, 1977).

Implementation

Lovitt (1984) suggests the following steps for implementing a cost response system in which tokens are taken away for breaking class rules.
1. Identify the target behaviors.
2. Discuss class rules with the students and remind them to follow the rules.
3. Give each student a cup holding 10 tokens at the beginning of the period.
4. The students are told that one token will be lost each time the rule is not followed.
5. Students must have six tokens at the end of the period to earn their reward (i.e. snack, sticker, free time).
6. Students should be told that occasionally there will be a "surprise day" and those who have the most tokens will be given a bonus. (Students are not told when "surprise days" are scheduled.

Research

Response cost has been used successfully in applied settings because it quickly suppresses problem behaviors. Studies report that response cost has reduced violent behaviors of psychiatric patients (Winkler, 1970), aggressive statements and tardiness of predelinquent boys (Phillips, 1968; Phillips et al., 1971) and rule violations in classrooms (Iwata & Bailey, 1974). Much research on response cost shows that inappropriate behaviors can be reduced by taking away only a few tokens or a few minutes of free or recess time. Taking away small units seems to be more effective than taking away a larger quantity. Whatever is taken away, however, must be valuable to the student. Current research seems to indicate that it is more effective to take away something that the student has earned (Lovitt, 1984).

Response cost should be combined with reinforcement of desired alternative behaviors. In fact, response cost may be used on a temporary basis to reduce inappropriate behaviors while the desired behaviors are being strengthened.

Systematic Desensitization

Target Behavior

AFFECTIVE
Coping with anxiety

Description

The purpose of systematic desensitization is to teach a child to cope with anxiety. Many negative or problem behaviors are exhibited because they have been paired with stimuli that elicit them. The rationale for systematic desensitization suggests that if problem behaviors can be learned through this procedure, then more favorable responses can also be learned. Systematic desensitization incorporates information giving, relaxation training, establishment of hierarchies, counterconditioning procedures, positive self-talk, and active participation.

Implementation

Olson (1982) suggests the following steps for implementing systematic desensitization.

1. Tell the student how behaviors are learned.
2. Identify factors that are producing anxiety in the student's life.
3. Teach the child to alternately relax and tense various muscle groups in a systematic way.
4. Teach the student the proper way of breathing for relaxation.
5. List the anxiety-producing stimuli in order, from most anxiety producing to least anxiety producing. The student should be involved in this ranking process.
6. Tell the child to relax using the relaxation exercises. Then present the stimuli from the lowest level of the ranked hierarchy. The idea is to pair a pleasurable response (relaxation) with the stimulus that typically elicits anxiety.
7. Positive self-talk, such as "So what if I cry in school, I still am an important person" can be verbalized by the student when he is relaxing and thinking of the unpleasant stimuli.
8. The relaxation and self-talk should continue until the highest level of the hierarchy is presented to the child. The time frame for introducing the next higher level of anxiety is determined by how relaxed the child remains. Usually the whole hierarchy of stimuli is not presented in one session.
9. It is helpful to cue the student during class time to use relaxation and positive self-talk during anxious moments.

Research

For two years Lupin (1977) used a systematic desensitization program with an emotionally handicapped student. Initially this student had little self confidence and could not perform satisfactory work. Relaxation tapes and positive self-talk were used to assist the student. She progressed from attending the regular classroom for lunch and music (stimuli that produced the least anxiety in her hierarchy) to language arts and math (the most anxiety producing).

In the past, desensitization was not a common technique for teachers to use due to lack of training. Commercial programs, such as Lupin's Peace, Harmony, Awareness makes these techniques more readily available for teachers to implement.

The Timer Game

Target Behaviors

AFFECTIVE
  Keeping hands in right place
COMPLIANCE
  Sitting properly
  Staying in seat
  Staying on task
  Working quietly

Description

This intervention is used in many classrooms. It is based on the idea that time devices can be helpful in managing student behavior. A kitchen timer is set for variable time intervals throughout the school day. Whenever the bell rings, students are reinforced for exhibiting the target behavior and the timer is reset. This technique may be used in conjunction with a more general management plan, such as a token economy.

Implementation

Lovitt (1984) suggests several steps for implementing this intervention.

1.   Identify the target behavior.
2.   Discuss the identified behavior with the students.
3.   Place a timer in front of the room. Set the timer for intervals ranging from 0 to 40 minutes throughout the day.
4.   When the timer goes off, place a point or tally next to the names of those children who are exhibiting the target behavior. Their names may be written on the blackboard or in a special log book.
5.   Reset the timer and resume the class activity.
6.   Periodically the students should be given time to redeem their points for various prizes or privileges (i.e. line leader, assistant physical education coach, stickers).

Research

The Timer Game was effective when used with low achieving children from lower socio-economic urban homes. These students were mostly fourth graders who attended a remedial classroom after their regular school day (Wolf, Hanley, King, Lachowicz & Giles, 1970). This technique has also been effective when used with individual students for certain parts of the day.

32

Token Reinforcement System

Target Behaviors

ACADEMIC IMPROVEMENT
  Improving skills
  Increasing accuracy of work
  Increasing number of assignments completed
  Increasing skills acquired
AFFECTIVE
  Cooperating with peers
  Keeping hands in right place
  Participating in group
  Promoting positive relationships among peers
  Verbalizing positively
AGGRESSION
  Maintaining nonaggressive behavior
COMPLIANCE
  Completing assignments
  Raising hand
  Sitting properly
  Staying on task
  Working quietly

Description

A token is an item such as points, chips, checkmarks, or play money that is paid to a student immediately following the occurrence of a target behavior. The tokens themselves have little intrinsic value. They acquire value, however, when they are later exchanged for a desired object or activity. A classroom store may be set up where children can spend their tokens to "purchase" a preferred item. A reward menu may also be hung listing privileges that can be earned with tokens (i.e. using the computer, listening to a radio, going to the media center).

A token reinforcement system should be simple and functional. Checkmark tokens are often the easiest to use in a classroom setting. Each student is given a point card with 100 squares. (see Figure 4). The target behaviors are listed on the back of the point card. The teacher puts checks on the card as they are earned. Verbal praise (i.e. I like the way you're working quietly) should be paired with the token or checkmark so that eventually only the social reinforcement will be needed to maintain the target behaviors (Mercer & Mercer, 1985).

Implementation

The following guidelines have been suggested for planning and using a token system (Blackham & Silberman, 1980).

33

Figure 4.

Sample Point Card for Teacher Use.

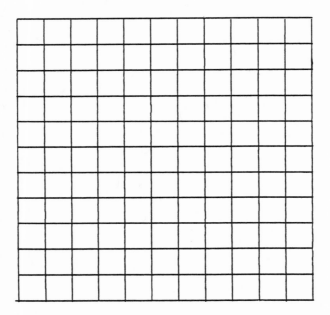

1. The target behaviors that earn tokens must be clearly understood.
2. Tokens must be exchanged for reinforcers that are appealing to the student. It is helpful to have these reinforcers only available within the token system.
3. The number of tokens earned must correspond to the effort required for performing the behavior. For example, if a student has a very difficult time remembering to raise his hand before speaking he should earn more tokens, more often for doing so. He would earn fewer tokens, less often for behaviors that are less difficult to exhibit.
4. The system should be designed so that students compete with themselves rather than others.

Listed below are some additional suggestions for implementing a token reinforcement system.

1. Tokens should be given immediately following appropriate behavior.
2. A place to keep the tokens should be provided.
3. A token should never be given to a student who asks for one.
4. Tokens should not be given to a student who is exhibiting an inappropriate behavior.
5. An appreciation of how the token reinforcement system relates to real life should be developed.
6. The token system should be continually evaluated and refined and gradually faded into a social reinforcement system.
7. It is better to give too many tokens than to give too few.

Research

Token reinforcement systems are often used in behavior modification programs. They have proven themselves effective for increasing a great variety of desired student behaviors. Many investigators report success with this intervention. Brown, Bellamy, Perlmutter, Sackowitz, and Sontag (1972) obtained increases in production rate using token reinforcement systems. Increased work rates with mentally retarded students were demonstrated using a "points exchangeable for activity reinforcers" token system (Zimmerman, Stuckey, Garlick, & Miller, 1969). A "combination of social and token reinforcement" system also produced increased work rates (Brown, Johnson, Gadberry, & Fenrick, 1971). Jason and Rebeck (1984) report the effectiveness of token reinforcement for reducing excessive television viewing. In this study tokens were earned for prosocial activities (e.g. coloring, doing homework, clearing the table, playing games, playing with friends, etc.). Additionally, Fabry, Mayhew, and Hanson (1984) describe the effectiveness of token systems for improving academic skills such as learning new vocabulary words.

The Turtle Technique for Managing Aggression

Target Behaviors

AGGRESSION
   Demonstrating nonviolent behaviors
   Keeping hands and legs in right place
   Maintaining nonaggressive behavior

Description

   This technique assumes that elementary school students can be taught to manage certain aggressive behaviors. It also assumes the necessity of relying on students to help change the behaviors of their peers. This intervention combines encouragement, support, teacher feedback, and reinforcement to prevent aggression in the classroom (Lovitt, 1984).

Implementation

   The following steps have been suggested for introducing and using the Turtle Technique (Lovitt, 1984).

   1.   Read the following story to the students.

        Little Turtle was very upset about going to school. When he was there he got into trouble because he fought with his mates. Other turtles teased, bumped, or hit him. He then became angry and started fights. The teacher then punished him. One day he met the big old tortoise who told him that his shell was the secret answer to many problems. The tortoise told Little Turtle to withdraw into his shell whenever he felt angry, and rest until he felt better. Little Turtle tried it the next day and it worked. He no longer became angry or started fights, his teacher now smiled at him, and he began to like school. (p. 251)

   2.   Teach the turtle response to the students. (arms and legs are pulled in close to the body and heads are put down on the desks). Tell the student to imagine he is a turtle withdrawing into his shell.

   3.   Teach the students to use the turtle response in four situations.
        a.   When the student foresees that an aggressive incident is about to occur.
        b.   When the student is angry with himself.
        c.   When the teacher says "turtle."
        d.   When a peer says "turtle."

36

4. Teach the students to alternately tense and relax muscles while in the turtle position.

5. Provide problem-solving instruction including the process of generating problem coping strategies and predicting consequences for choices made.

Research

Many teacher-administered, externally controlled techniques for helping behavior disordered students control their impulses and overcome behavioral deficits have been developed (O'Leary & O'Leary, 1972). One limitation to these techniques has been the return of the behavior to nearly pretreatment levels when the treatment is terminated (Schneider & Dolnick, 1976). An alternative approach, self-control behavior modification procedures, has been suggested as a possible solution (Thoreson & Mahoney, 1974). Using a self-control approach such as the Turtle Technique involves teaching children strategies that they can use to control their own inappropriate behavior with minimal teacher intervention. These self-control methods have proven successful with both behavior disordered and normal children (Drabman, Spitalnik & O'Leary, 1973; Thoreson & Mahoney, 1974). A specific study on the turtle method revealed that 11 primary age students in self-contained classes for the emotionally disturbed were less aggressive after implementing this intervention (Schneider & Dolnick, 1976).

PART II

RELATED TOPICS

Knowledge of these general strategies and specific techniques for managing student behavior will increase the likelihood of maintaining an effective classroom environment. An understanding of reinforcement, punishment, and behavior measurement is also recommended. Therefore, the remainder of this text presents an overview of these three topics. It is hoped the reader will synthesize the information and use it successfully to promote positive behavior changes.

Reinforcement:

Constructing and Maintaining Behavior/s

The use of positive reinforcement relates to one of the fundamental laws of behavior that has reliably demonstrated its effect across a multitude of arrangements. In everyday life, reinforcement assumes many forms, and occurs naturally as a person behaves.

This section describes some of the fundamentals of using reinforcement and schedules of reinforcement to teach and maintain behaviors. There are many strategies and tactics that can be used to teach students new responses. Teachers are provided with the concept of reinforcement that can be used in a classroom. In fact, teachers may view this as a discussion on how to enhance classroom curriculum by using positive reinforcement.

Students are typically motivated for many types of reinforcement. This can easily work to a teacher's advantage. The following is a list of reinforcers used to motivate students to perform.

1. Attention: Teacher praise[1] principal praise, and/or peer pressure.

2. Opportunity to perform chores: Messenger, clean blackboard, take out garbage, stay after school to help the teacher, helping another student.

3. Earning a desirable activity: Free play, computer time, art, music, extra P. E., reading a magazine, talking with a friend or show 'n' tell.

4. Parties: Earning a weekly popcorn party.

5. Movies: Earning a weekly movie.

---

[1] Whenever possible use specific language that describes an action within a particular place and time. For example, when dispensing reinforcement, state to the student exactly what he did to earn it and when it occurred.

6. Bonus points: Earning extra homework to get bonus points toward a higher grade. Bonus points may also be earned to avoid taking a particular quiz, to eliminate a homework assignment for a particular evening, to get a sticker, to get a "good day" note, to have name placed on the outside door of the classroom with a slogan of recognition underneath.

7. Choice of academic activity: This procedure allows a student to choose when he works on a particular assignment. For example, if a student has regularly produced completed accurate work to criteria, he could be asked to choose which independent work assignment to do first.

8. 500 Club: The number 500 is arbitrary, but the principle applies. Have the students keep a daily tally of the number of assignments they complete. Randomly verify their count. Put a running total under their names on a publicly posted list. When a student obtains a certain number of completed assignments (i.e., 500), then he earns a membership card to the 500 Club. Membership entitles the student to certain desirable activities such as choosing when they do certain kinds of independent academic assignments, being a peer tutor, and having the opportunity to arrange special social arrangements for other students who have entered the 500 Club.

9. Academic Athletes (Tenenbaum and Wolking, 1981): Teacher publicly posts the best achievements during the week of all or certain students. This could include the highest reading rate, the most math problems accurately completed in a certain amount of time, the number of consecutive days/weeks that 90% or more students received above average grades on spelling tests, students who have completed their homework, and any other academically related behavior that is especially noteworthy. Each day prior to any instruction the teacher provides the students with a "prep rally." The teacher points out how well all the students or some of the students did on a particular task. The teacher draws attention to the principles of becoming a good athlete (i.e., daily practice, learning new skills, measuring performance). For example, the teacher asks the students "how did Pete Rose learn to become a great hitter?" The teacher then waits for replies or then states "daily practice, learning to be accurate." The teacher may wish to use a different sports figure each day. The teacher then applies these principles to doing academic work.

10. Primary reinforcement: This involves the provision of some biologically pleasing event that is made contingent on a behavior. For example, the teacher gives a child a piece of candy when work is completed. This method can be very effective. However, it is a low level reinforcer and it typically does not occur within a natural school environment.

41

Student behavior is the test of whether or not a reinforcer is effective. Behavior observations before and during reinforcement provides the teacher with data regarding the effectiveness. Some children who have not experienced certain kinds of reinforcement will not be motivated to perform. For example, if a student has not had the experience of playing with a computer, then earning computer time may be an inadequate motivation. Initially, the teacher may wish to expose the student to the reinforcer without applying a contingency. This is also known as reinforcement sampling (Ayllon and Azrin, 1968). This is similar to the old adage, "you have to give a little to get a little." When the student begins to enjoy the potential reinforcer, it is time to arrange a contingency to earn the new reinforcer.

Schedules of Reinforcement or When to Reinforce

Fixed and Variable Intervals

Using fixed and variable intervals refers to the schedule of reinforcement that is being used. Fixed interval requires that a behavior receives reinforcement when it occurs after a certain amount of time elapses. For example, after 10 minutes if Fred is sitting in his seat, he earns 1 minute of computer time. A variable interval requires that a behavior receives reinforcement within a random amount of time. For example, Fred receives free time if sitting in his seat when a kitchen timer rings. The bell may ring at any time within the designated interval.

Uses of Interval Schedules

Interval schedules can be used concurrently and/or singularly. They have widespread use across most environments. Teachers may wish to use a fixed interval schedule within their daily classroom structure. For example, a kitchen timer may be set to ring every 30 minutes. The teacher then praises a handful of students who are working quietly at their seats. When dealing with more severe behaviors, the timer is set to go off more frequently. For example, if a student is on task when a timer rings every 5 minutes, the student earns a point toward free play.

Fixed interval schedules are frequently used to help students learn and maintain a new behavior. Students on this schedule usually produce a low frequency of responses until the interval is near. Typically, the responses accelerate just as the interval approaches.

A variable interval of reinforcement requires more management of the teacher's time than does the fixed interval. This schedule is used when a teacher wishes to maintain a steady rate of responding. When this schedule is initially introduced, the teacher may wish to be certain that the amount of time before reinforcement is dispensed will not be longer than what the student is capable of waiting. Thus, a teacher may wish to set a timer to ring within 5 to 10 minutes when first starting this schedule. When a stable rate of responding has been obtained, the timer can be set to go off randomly within an increased upper limit of time.

Concurrent Use of Fixed and Interval Schedules

The use of a variable interval usually produces a steady rate of behavior. Although the rate of behavior on this schedule is usually not as high as the rates obtained on a variable ratio (see ratio schedules), using a fixed and variable interval schedule students can learn to respond at a steady rate over a period of time. For example, if a teacher wishes for a student to be reinforced only on Fridays, then the two schedules could be used to allow for this. First, the teacher begins with reinforcing the student with points once every 30 minutes and within 30 minutes the teacher will provide praise to the student. At the end of 30 minutes, the student receives 10 minutes of an activity of his choosing within the classroom. When the student responds consistently the teacher begins to increase the amount of time on the two schedules. Thus, over a period of time, students can begin to receive the reinforcing event at the end of the week. When the students gain experience with this systematic arrangement the teacher can increase the interval. Also, the teacher may wish to reestablish a variable interval schedule for a particular behavior while the fixed interval schedule remains the same. Of course, this procedure could be reversed. In other words, the teacher keeps a variable interval in effect while manipulating the fixed interval when teaching new behaviors.

Advantages and Disadvantages of Fixed Intervals

A fixed interval schedule typically is used to shape certain behaviors and to increase the amount of time before a reinforcer is provided. A fixed interval is relatively easy to implement in terms of teacher time.

Fixed intervals in themselves, however, do not increase the probability that the student will exhibit the desired behavior throughout the interval. For example, if a fixed interval of 10 minutes is in effect, then the student is reinforced for exhibiting the target behavior soon after the 10 minute interval has elapsed. Thus, it does not matter what the student was doing prior to the signal of the 10-minute interval. For this reason fixed intervals are good for **shaping** or strengthening a behavior.

Advantages and Disadvantages of Variable Intervals

Variable intervals are very potent for producing a steady rate of behavior and are easy to implement. Variable intervals help to teach generalization of behavior. This is done through reinforcing the student only at times that cannot be predicted by the student. In other words, the student must be performing the desired behavior to be reinforced. Since, however, the onset of the reinforcer is not predictable, the student is apt to maintain a steady rate of responding to increase the likelihood of receiving the reinforcer.

This schedule tends to teach low rate of responding. This could be detrimental if a teacher is attempting to have students perform certain kinds of computations at a high rate.

Advantages and Disadvantages of Using a Concurrent Fixed and Variable Interval Schedule of Reinforcement

This arrangement typically will shape behavior quickly and will maintain it at a steady rate. The teacher can also use this schedule combination to train students to come under the control of a variable interval of reinforcement. For example, a teacher who has a fixed interval of 30' and intermittently reinforces behavior within that 30' can begin to increase the 30' contingency. As the 30' contingency increases, the teacher also increases the number of times the students are reinforced. This procedure can be stretched out until the student/s are on a fixed interval of 5 days, but the teacher continues to intermittently reinforce the students.

Variable schedules have an advantage over fixed schedules, because of their resistance to extinction. That is, behaviors tend to maintain longer in the absence of reinforcement when under a variable schedule. This principle is advantageous to a teacher, because he can become less systematic in providing reinforcement. This is not to say that reinforcement should be totally discontinued.

Typically, behaviors on this schedule will remain at a low rate. Thus, a variable ratio schedule yields a higher rate of student performance.

Ratio Schedule

Ratio schedules, unlike interval schedules, use a performance criterion to produce a functional effect. In other words, a certain number of behaviors must occur before an environmental response is produced that will maintain its occurrence.

Fixed Ratio Schedule

The fixed ratio schedule produces a high steady rate of responding. This schedule produces a reinforcing event when a certain number of predetermined responses occur. For example, when Fred raises his hand three times, the teacher will call on him. Teachers typically use this schedule when teaching a new skill. During the initial stages of acquisition many teachers will praise a student for each correct answer that is given. This is called a fixed ratio of one or a continuous reinforcement schedule.

Variable Ratio Schedule

The variable ratio schedule produces the highest performance rate of all schedules. Under this schedule the teacher produces a reinforcer within a certain number of student responses that cannot be predicted by the student. For example, a variable ratio of 20 produces the occasion that within 20 responses, the student will have access to the reinforcing event. The student learns that he will never be reinforced unless he is performing. And since the reinforcer cannot be predicted, the student usually continues to work at a high rate. The reinforcer is performance based, therefore, the more quickly a certain number of responses has occurred, the sooner the student will be reinforced.

This schedule teaches the student to "gamble" on good behavior. The variable ratio schedule is typically used by gambling casinos. It is easy to see the effects that this schedule has on motivation.

Combination of Schedules

Typically in a school setting students are put on fixed interval and fixed ratio schedules of reinforcement. They are usually required to finish a certain amount of work within a particular time period. This combination schedule typically produces slow, steady responding if the reinforcer is related to the fixed interval schedule. This is usually the case. When a student hands in an assignment, this can mark the end of a time period and thus a change in the environment is produced (e.g., a different worksheet or going to lunch, etc.). However, some students who do not produce a certain amount of work still get reinforced because they have met the requirements of the fixed interval schedule. For example, if a teacher gives the student a worksheet at 11:30 a.m., regardless of how many problems the student completes, at 12:00 noon that student typically goes to lunch.

At times it would be more appropriate to use a fixed and/or variable interval schedule, but teachers usually want students to perform quickly and accurately. The variable ratio schedule allows for this to occur since it is a movement based schedule. A certain number of responses must occur before the student is reinforced. Whenever a rate of performance is reinforced, one can expect the behavior to increase over time. In this schedule, the student can predict that behavior must be occurring before it can be reinforced. Variable ratio schedules maintain a behavior over a long period of time. As stated earlier, this schedule can be used to reliably produce a high rate of performance. Moreover, students tend to remember the skill(s) they are taught.

Since a teacher needs to know exactly when each student has produced the desired number of responses, teacher demand in terms of time is great without some electronic monitoring device. A fixed interval along with a fixed ratio schedule may best be used during the initial phases of setting up classroom structure. Also, the teacher should build in surprise reinforcers to help maintain a variable ratio schedule. In this scenerio, a certain number of responses must occur within a particular time period. For example, students must do 10/15 math problems within five minutes, so that they can receive teacher praise. Sometimes, the teacher may surprise the students by dispensing a novel reinforcer to those who have completed a certain amount of work. In other words, the teacher "Catches them being good performers."

The difficulty with setting up a systematic schedule is the frequency involved in dispensing the reinforcement. The teacher should determine which schedule to use and how often the students will need to be reinforced. Only by a trial and error procedure and taking measures can a teacher decide which schedule is necessary for student success.

The ultimate goal is to eliminate the need for contrived schedules. Initially, however, a schedule should be selected that is productive and easily modified so that it approaches a variable ratio; these yield a high rate of steady behavior which is resistant to being forgotten.

Punishment

Punishment is defined as a procedure that eliminates or decreases the frequency or duration of behavior(s). Punishment works in the reverse of reinforcement.

There are varying levels of punishment. Each can be used effectively (Foxx, 1982). However, prior to implementing a behavior reduction procedure with punishment, one should provide the occasion to reinforce some alternative response. Initially, the reinforcement density must be greater for the alternative response. Punishment should not be administered without some other behavior being reinforced. The concept of "behavior pairs" (Lindsley, 1980) is most applicable when any punishment procedure is used. When choosing a behavior to suppress, some other behavior is targeted to be constructed or increased.

This chapter will cover several punishment procedures that teachers of regular and mildly handicapped students can use. For a more extensive review of punishment procedures for students with severe behavior disorders, the reader is referred to Decreasing Behaviors (Foxx, 1982).

When to Punish?

Punishment is typically used to eliminate and/or decrease the frequency and/or duration of some maladaptive response. Prior to implementing a punishment procedure the teacher should have provided the student with positive reinforcement for appropriate responding. Only when the use of reinforcement has proven to be ineffective does a teacher consider the use of punishment. Teachers of children with severe behavior problems may wish to begin a punishment procedure for behaviors that are life threatening and/or impinge on the safety and property of others.

When a punishment procedure is implemented, it is carried out quickly and the student is placed in an environment where he/she contacts immediate positive contingencies. The frequency of punishing stimuli is **never** greater than the number of reinforcers that the student receives.

Effective teachers of students with severe behavior disorders implement the 95/5 rule. This means that for 95% of an instructional day the student maintains contact with positive contingencies. For five percent of the day he receives aversive stimuli. When punishment exceeds five percent, new interventions are constructed.

Disadvantages of Punishment

If punishment is not administered correctly, the targeted behavior has the potential of accelerating. Unfortunately, punishing consequences are the only means by which some children receive attention. Thus, punishment then becomes a reinforcer. The importance of collecting data cannot be understated, when considering this possible side effect.

47

When punishment is given without regard to reinforcing other behaviors or providing the student with alternative responses, then the student either learns to escape or avoid the aversive setting. Many students with behavior disorders typically develop escape and avoidance maneuvers. This class of behavior is directly related to their frequency of receiving aversive stimuli within a school system. The importance of reinforcing new behaviors and/or different behaviors is paramount and must be part of any punishment procedure.

Punishment often serves to reinforce a teacher's actions rather than provide the student with help. When first punishing a student, the behavior being punished will frequently disappear for some period of time. Thus, the teacher is reinforced because an unwanted stimuli (behavior) has been removed from the environment. When the behavior reappears, a cycle is often established. This scenerio typifies what occurs when many students are paddled in school systems. The teacher and/or principal believe that the paddling has worked because the student within a period of time stops exhibiting the behaviors that brought forth the paddling. Paddling in itself does not guarantee that a child will stop a behavior from occurring. In fact, when paddling and/or any other aversive event is used without reinforcing other behaviors, the student learns to become devious and gets better at practicing inappropriate behaviors.

Developing a Punishment Procedure

Designing a punishment procedure requires careful planning and a commitment to follow through both negatively and positively. Begin by taking baseline (see measurement section on taking baseline) of the behavior you wish to eliminate or decrease. Always measure the effectiveness of your punishment procedure. Some students have been referred to the principal 30 to 40 times a year to be spanked. Obviously these principals did not have a measure of their effectiveness.

When baseline is established, decide which procedure will be implemented. Also, determine the number of days a procedure will be used before it is changed. A daily record is maintained of the number of times the punishment procedure had to be implemented. As soon as the decision has been reached on the procedure to be used, the behavior to be reinforced is selected.

The following is a listing of punishment procedures from the most mild to the most restrictive within a public school setting for regular and for the mildly handicapped student. The procedures listed here should never be used longer than it is necessary. There are side effects to punishment procedures that can be circumvented when they are used appropriately.

Ignoring

This teacher response requires little time to implement, yet many people find it difficult to carry out. This procedure is used when a mildly disruptive behavior occurs and the teacher does not attend to it. Mildly disruptive refers to such behaviors as talking out of turn, interrupting a conversation and calling out. In order for ignoring to work, the teacher must not give the student any indication that the student is being ignored. This requires the teacher to be a good actor. Proximity and eye contact should be avoided.

When a teacher implements an ignoring procedure it is suggested that the teacher provide other students with reinforcement for performing the expected behaviors. For example, if a student's calling out behavior is being ignored, the teacher would begin praising other students for sitting quietly and/or for raising their hand before speaking. When the student being ignored displays the appropriate behavior, the teacher dispenses reinforcement to that student.

When dealing with young or naive students, the teacher may need to state the expected behavior and related contingency before ignoring can be used effectively. For example, if a child calls out, the teacher may state, "As soon as you raise your hand quietly, I will help you." The teacher then calls on students demonstrating the expected behavior and explains why they are being assisted. The teacher may state, "Fred, you have a good quiet hand raise, how can I help you?" As soon as the calling out student demonstrates a quiet hand raise, the teacher offers immediate reinforcement.

Some situations may require more powerful forms of reinforcement. For example, to reinforce in seat behavior, the teacher may wish to ignore out of seat behavior while providing a surprise for those students who have been sitting in their seats. The teacher may also wish to vocally remind the in seat students of the good things that are planned for them within the near future. It must be explained that only students who are doing a good job of sitting in their seats will get to participate.

Disadvantages of Ignoring

Certain behaviors are simply not meant to be ignored. For example, if a student is about to throw a desk or is ready to inflict harm on himself, a physical intervention may be more appropriate. Ignoring is difficult for many teachers to use. Therefore, it must be an all or none treatment procedure. By not following through consistently, the teacher can potentially increase an unwanted behavior to intolerable levels. For example, if a student has been calling out and the teacher finally calls on the student after two minutes, then that student has begun to learn to increase calling out at least to a two minute duration. The next time, the student calls out he maintains the response for 2 or 2½ minutes and then the teacher acknowledges the student. When the teacher begins to reinforce the student on a variable ratio schedule, the behavior becomes contingent on a very powerful schedule (highly resistant to extinction).

Verbal Reprimands

Most educators and/or parents have probably provided their share of reprimands to children. This is a very common form of punishment that can be delivered effectively and quickly. People who use verbal reprimands should regard two simple principles. First, measure its effectiveness and second, reinforce positive alternative behaviors.

When providing a student with a reprimand it has been demonstrated that eye contact and proximity with a loud harsh voice can be used as an effective behavior suppression technique. When giving a reprimand the teacher should provide the student with direct eye contact within arm's length and vocalize with a higher than usual pitch. Reprimands are most effective when delivered quickly and take no longer than one minute (Blanchard & Johnson, 1982). A reprimand should state the emotional consequence it has on the delivering person. The expected behavior is also communicated. For example, when reprimanding a student for being late to class, the teacher may say "When you are late you disrupt my teaching and the other students. This makes me angry." The teacher then follows up with "You have demonstrated in the past that you can be reliable and on time to my class. Tardiness is unlike you. In the future I know you will continue to be on time." Once these things are stated, nothing more needs to be said. The next day, and for several days thereafter, the teacher seeks the opportunity to praise and/or provide the student with a desirable consequence for being on time to class.

This technique is only effective for those students who have a history of aversive consequences that were consistently delivered after a reprimand. Only by collecting data on this procedure can a teacher know for sure if the procedure is effective.

Reprimands should not be used as threats. In fact, a student should never be threatened. Following through on the stated consequence or reprimand is very important. An example of a reprimand is, "Do not get out of your seat!" or "Walk with your hands at your sides!" When reprimands contain threats, the teacher sets up a situation whereby the student is likely to challenge the teacher. Furthermore, when threats are not carried through, the reprimand becomes very weak in its effectiveness.

To illustrate this point, consider a classroom teacher who threatens her students 16 times in an hour. Their behaviors are as disruptive following a reprimand as they are prior to it. The teacher finally sends one student to the principal's office. The rest of the class exhibits more acceptable behavior and returns to their work. Within 18 to 20 minutes, a crescendo again builds in the classroom. This time the teacher makes 19 threats before another student is sent to be paddled. The students have the teacher on an interesting schedule of reinforcement. They have learned that the teacher provides nonaversive reprimands and threats; it was not necessary to comply with her requests until after 18 to 20 threats had been issued.

Differential Reinforcement of Other Behaviors (DRO)

DRO is a procedure which may be regarded more as a positive repertoire building procedure than as a straight punishment procedure. The title is descriptive in that the teacher seeks and reinforces other behaviors that are different from the behavior he wishes to eliminate.

For example, the student who calls out frequently can be reinforced when he is engaged in some desirable behavior. Catch the child being good and/or complying to some demand and provide positive reinforcement.

Disadvantages of DRO

The difficulty of using a DRO schedule is similar to those found under ignoring. At times, some behaviors cannot be ignored while waiting for a positive response to occur. Also, some children do not have a large enough repertoire of frequently occurring responses that is desirable for a teacher to reinforce. In these cases, the teacher may have to model correct responding or use a shaping procedure.

For some children, reinforcing some other behavior will not guarantee that they will generalize to the undesirable response. For example, if you are training a student not to call out in class, by reinforcing him for standing in line appropriately, the odds are that he will not generalize to calling out. DRO has its greatest effectiveness if the student is being reinforced frequently across settings and tasks.

Differential Reinforcement of Incompatible Behavior (DRI)

This behavior suppression technique is used when an incompatible behavior is reinforced. The principle is similar to the physics axiom, that two objects cannot occupy the same space at the same time. For example, if a child is calling out, opportunities must be found to reinforce the child for sitting quietly. A student cannot sit quietly and call out at the same time. As the incompatible behavior increases in frequency, the problem behavior will automatically decrease.

Disadvantages of DRI

This procedure is excellent and strongly recommended; its only disadvantage is that an incompatible response may not be easily accessible. In this case, the teacher must construct the repertoire.

51

Response Cost

The response cost procedure is similar to that used by law enforcement agencies. When an infraction is made on the highway, fines can be assessed. Response cost is used to decrease a behavior through the removal of some portion of the total number of reinforcers.

Response cost typically consists of a reinforcement program in which generalized reinforcers are used. Tokens, points or money can fall in the category of generalized reinforcers. The teacher in this procedure removes some amount of the reinforcer contingent on some behavior targeted to be eliminated or decreased. For example, if a student was on a fixed interval schedule of 10, every 10 minutes he would receive 10 points on a point card. The points may later be traded in for one of several options (i.e., stickers, extra computer time, visit with favorite teacher, etc.). If the teacher wishes to decrease the number of times a student hits a classmate, she may choose to fine the student 2 points each time it occurs. Of course, this arrangement should be constructed prior to implementation of the response cost program.

Response cost has been shown to be very effective in eliminating such behaviors as: impulsivity, hyperactivity, hitting, cursing, biting, tardiness, increasing seat work accuracy, time on task and noncompliance. Response cost has the advantage of providing the teacher with a natural opportunity to reinforce appropriate behavior. Points or any other reinforcers serve as a natural stimulus to remind the teacher to dispense the reinforcement for correct behaviors.

The system requires effort and consistency by the teachers. Prior to using a response cost system, it is necessary to demonstrate that the reinforcement can be delivered accurately and quickly. Moreover, the cost or fine must be levied quickly and without fanfare.

Disadvantages of Response Cost

Response cost typically works well with higher functioning students. A fair amount of effort is required to implement this procedure and a commitment to levy fines when appropriate. The use of response cost has been well documented and its effectiveness has been demonstrated.

Time Out

This is one of the most widely used intervention strategies and is probably over used. Time out is nothing more than removing a child from a reinforcing event. Usually this occurs when a student is misbehaving.

Caution

Time out should only be used when positive reinforcement and evoking a modeling response has been exhausted. It should only be used by trained teachers. When using time out be sure that the event from which the child is removed was reinforcing to him. Simply removing the child does not mean that he will comply in order to reengage in the activity from which he was removed. Only by keeping a record of the occurrences of the misbehavior will the teacher know for sure if a time out procedure has been effective.

Procedure

Step one is to ask the child to move his seat from the desk or table for one minute and to sit quietly. Place the student facing the other children. This **cues** the teacher to begin reinforcing other children for appropriate behavior. The teacher may want to begin **hamming** it up with the other students. Time out should never be longer than 30 minutes. In fact, one to five minutes should be the norm. The last 15 seconds of time is the most crucial. If for example, a student is told that he is to be in time out for five minutes, remove the student if in the last 15 seconds he exhibits correct responding (Foxx, 1982). If the student is still acting inappropriately, reset time out for one additional minute. Removal from time out is contingent on correct behavior for the duration of the last 15 seconds.

Step two is to remove the child from the classroom. This should only be done if a child is becoming so disruptive that he might cause injury or property destruction. Time out should not be used to get rid of a student, it is used to **train** students to perform in a desirable manner.

Some students will enter time out when asked by the teacher. If a student does not comply quickly (usually within five seconds), the teacher immediately and without any conflict guides the student to the time out spot. When a child is in time out, care should be taken to assure that the time out situation is not a reinforcer for the student.

Except in very extreme situations, time out should be done within the classroom. In those unfortunate times when a student must be removed, the 15 second rule during the last minute is employed. Remember, time out should be no longer than 30 minutes.

Many students are chronically sent to the principal's office. They typically engage in conversations with their peers while waiting a half hour or more to see the principal. The principal's secretary often greets the student with some kind of comment like "a day wouldn't be complete if you didn't arrive." Although this is typically aimed at embarrassing the youngster, it may also serve as a reinforcer. When sending a student to the principal, it is a good idea to have a procedure developed in which the student does not have access to any stimulating conversations or exposure to a novel environment. The principal or any other disciplinarian should be

53

ready to deal with the problem quickly and to return the student to the environment in which he committed the misbehavior.

A student returning from a time out situation should serve as a cue for the teacher to catch the child performing some appropriate behavior and communicate that he is now acting appropriately.

Negative Reinforcement

Negative reinforcement is typically used to accelerate a behavior. In most chapters on behavior analysis it can typically be found in behavior increasing sections. It is included under the punishment section, because it is used contingent on a behavior that is targeted for deceleration.

Negative reinforcement is the removal of an aversive event that is made contingent on a desirable and/or adaptive response. For example, when training eye contact to an autistic student, the teacher can place her hand on either side of the student's head and exert a little pressure. As soon as the eyes make contact with the teacher, the teacher immediately lets go and reinforces the student (Rolider & Van Houten, 1985). Negative reinforcement is used by a teacher when she turns the lights off in a classroom to get the students to sit quietly. As soon as the class is quiet, the lights are put back on.

A teacher may wish to employ the power of negative reinforcement by simply removing a task from a student until the desired behavior surfaces. To do this the teacher simply removes a task that has typically been associated with a reinforcing event. Tell the child as soon as he is doing whatever it is you want the student to do (i.e., sitting quietly), the task will be given back. As soon as the student returns to performing the desired behavior, the task is returned. Reinforcement should be given immediately following corrected behavior.

Some Ethical Considerations

Punishment should never be used without the opportunity to reinforce an alternative response. If one does not exist, then the teacher is obligated to build a repertoire of competing responses before any punishment procedure is implemented.

For additional information regarding the use of punishment, Decreasing Behaviors of Severely Retarded and Autistic Persons by Richard M. Foxx (1982) provides an excellent review of punishment procedures and their ethical considerations.

Measurement

At a recent curriculum conference the Commissioner of Education for the state of Florida, Ralph Turlington, remarked, "No one would pay to see a ball game if no one kept score." This remark was used to illustrate the importance for all educators to begin measuring student outcome.

The use of measurement is viewed as a tool in which teachers can visually view their effectiveness. This concept need not be complex or require a complicated set of procedures. To view teacher effectiveness, measurement strategies must have the following characteristics: The behavior that is to be measured is observable; the units of measurement (standard and absolute units of measurement such as seconds, minutes, feet, etc.) are independent of the subject's behavior (Johnston & Pennypacker, 1980); direct and continuous measurement is employed.

This section will discuss characteristics of measurement and some of the more common types of charts that are used to display behavioral data. The charts set the occasion for the teacher and/or student to view targeted behavior changes.

Observable Behavior

Before any measurement system is used, the teacher defines the behavior that is to be measured. The behavior should have a beginning and ending point. The teacher also determines the environment and under which stimulus conditions the behavior occurs frequently enough so that it can be measured reliably.

Once the teacher has determined what is to be measured, she determines what type of information will be recorded. For example, will duration or frequency be used? The teacher can use baseline data to help make that decision. Baseline is describing the behavior in measurable units prior to the onset of an intervention. For example, suppose the teacher wanted to eliminate head banging in a 6 year old first grade student. She may wish to count the frequency in which head banging occurs while the child is in a particular environment (e.g., classroom) under certain type of conditions (e.g., being taught math or reading). The teacher also has the option of taking duration data (e.g., the time between head bangs).

The importance of baseline data cannot be overstated. Baseline is typically used to determine the effectiveness of a teaching tactic. The baseline data are compared to the intervention data.

Steady States

Baseline and intervention phases are determined by the stability of the data. Baseline information is collected until the teacher is able to predict the next data point. Once the trend is established and /or stable, it is time to begin the intervention phase.

Units of Measurement

Units of measurement are very important in measuring behavioral phenomena. Selected units should be absolute and standard. For example, rate per minute (frequency) is a standard and absolute measurement unit. Absolute means that the data is fixed in some natural method of occurrence (e.g., counting and/or latency). Standard unit means that the data is characterized as some unit of time. No behavior occurs without reference to time. No event occurs without some reference to time. Furthermore, a standard unit is an agreed upon unit that does not change. For example, one minute of time means exactly one minute of time no matter who interprets the data.

Putting It All Together

If a teacher wishes to decrease the frequency in which a student calls out in class, it must first be determined how often it occurs. To do this the teacher keeps a record of each time the student calls out without permission. After two to three days the teacher is able to determine the general trend in the data. The teacher plots this data on a chart as call outs per school day. An intervention strategy is selected. The intervention could consist of giving the student praise for raising his hand quietly before he speaks. The number of call outs are recorded in the same fashion as they were during baseline phase.

When the targeted behavior either meets or fails to meet the desired goal, the teacher makes a decision based on the data as to the next step taken. For example, if the intervention phase data depicts a student who has significantly reduced his call outs from the baseline data, then the teacher may wish to decrease the number of praises she is dispensing. If the data during the intervention phase has not changed to an acceptable level of performance, the teacher implements a different intervention.

Intervention data should be gathered for as long as it suggests improvement in the desired direction. But, if the rate of improvement is not suitable, the teacher is free to implement other arrangements. Keeping a measurement system allows the teacher to be objective and to make data based decisions.

Direct and Continuous

Direct and continuous measurement schemes have been the hallmark of the natural sciences. Behaviors should be measured directly. In order to do so, the teacher should define exactly what is to be measured in observable dimensions. Counting the frequency of hand raises is a direct measure, determining a person's I.Q. is not. Determining if someone is hallucinating without hearing is not a direct measure. Counting the number of times someone reports hallucinations is a direct measure of vocal reporting of hallucinations (this still does not mean that internal hallucinations are counted; instead it is the number of hallucination reports that are counted.)

Continuous measurement simply requires that the person constantly measures the occurrence or nonoccurrence of a behavior within a given period of time. Several behavior analysts suggest alternate schemes of behavior observations such as time sampling. It seems that measuring behavior as it unravels in relationship to time is very helpful, particularly for classroom teachers. For a more complete discussion on this issue the reader is referred to Strategies and Tactics of Human Behavioral Research (Johnston & Pennypacker, 1980).

Charts

The type of chart that is used to display data should be one that accurately describes the effects of your intervention. Charts are used to provide feedback to teachers, learners, administrators and parents. The population who will view the charts should be considered when determining the type of chart format to use.

The following is a pictorial of the more frequently occurring charts that are found in the classroom. A single set of data will be used across all charts so that the reader can view how charts effect the data that is being displayed.

Chart 1 - Equal Interval

This chart is found in almost every school and classroom. It is called equal interval, because the data points are of equal distance from one another. The chart below depicts a student's time on task during and after baseline. The **phase change line** is placed prior to the intervention data.

Chart #1

Duration of Time on Task

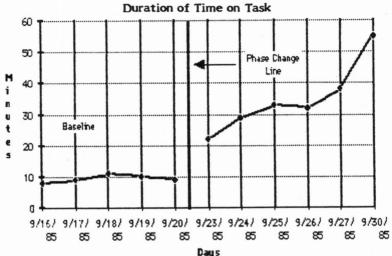

Line charts are economical and easy to use. Most people have an understanding of these charts. Furthermore, it is easy to draw in a trend line which can aid in the interpretation of the data. Chart #2 depicts the same set of data with a trend line drawn through it. A trend line can help the viewer visualize the amount of change that has occurred.

Chart #2

Duration of Time on Task

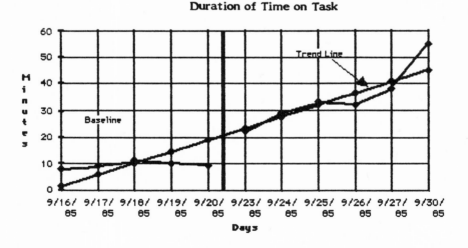

Column Chart

This graph is another common charting format. It is sometimes used to make the effect of the intervention appear more pronounced.

Chart #3

Duration of Time on Task

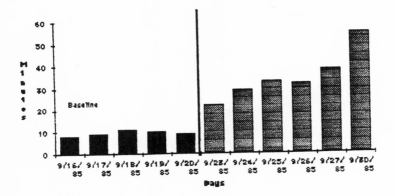

Pie Chart

This classic type of graph provides the viewer with the opportunity to see how a particular set of data relates to the whole. In this example, the viewer will be able to see the amount of time a student is on task in relationship to the total instructional time.

Chart #4

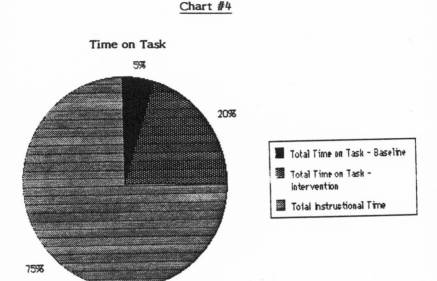

Time on Task

The pie chart is also an effective way to demonstrate intervention results. This chart may be used when it is necessary to display performance in relationship to a whole.

Log Charts

These are charts typically used within the scientific community. Advocates of Precision Teaching also use these charts to display academic performance over time.

Log charts are ratio charts. When the data are plotted on this chart, a "smoothing" effect occurs. That is, the data will more approximate a straight line. Log charts are good to use when the intent is to improve performance by large quantities. Ratio charts are also good for demonstrating behavioral change as a ratio and not as an absolute value. Thus, students who increase their performance from one movement per day to two per day experience a 100% increase. Students who increase from 80 per day to 100 per day experience a 25% increase. On a ratio chart this percent of change is more accurately depicted.

Chart #5

Duration of Time on Task

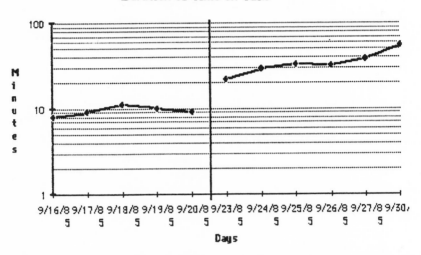

The data displayed on the log chart is characteristic of the tendency for these charts to "smooth" the data. The chart also does a good job of describing the ratio change from baseline to intervention phase. For example, if trend lines were drawn through the baseline and intervention phases, the viewer can see that the intervention phase doubled or increased the amount of on task performance by 100%.

Systematic measurement is the hallmark of all sciences. Without it technological and empirical discovery would be quite limited. Measurement is to progress as teaching is to learning. As Skip Berquam (1980), a famous Precision Teacher, once said, "Care enough to chart."

REFERENCES

Allen, V. L. (Ed.). (1976). Children as teachers: Theory and research on tutoring. New York: Academic Press.

Archer, A., Edgar, E. (1976). Teaching academic skills to mildly handicapped children. In S. Lavenbraun & J. Q. Affleck (Eds), Teaching mildly handicapped children in regular classes. Columbus, OH: Charles E. Merrill.

Ayllon, T., Azrin, N. H. (1968). Reinforcer sampling: A technique for increasing the behavior of mental patients. Journal of Applied Behavior Analysis, 1, 13-20.

Ayllon, T. & Azrin, N. H. (1968). The token economy: A motivational system for therapy and rehabilitation. New York: Appleton-Century-Crofts.

Azaroff, B. S., & Mayer, G. R. (1977). Applying behavior-analysis procedures with children and youth. New York: Holt, Rinehart, and Winston.

Azrin, N. H., & Holz, W. C. (1966). Punishment. In W. R. Honig (Ed.), Operant behavior: Areas of research and application. (pp. 380-447). New York: Appleton.

Barrish, H. H., Saunders, M., & Wolf, M. M. (1969). Good behavior game: Effects of individual contingencies for group consequences on disruptive behavior in a classroom. Journal of Applied Behavior Analysis, 2, 119-124.

Berquam, S. (1980). Personal communication. Paper presented at the Precision Teaching Conference, Orlando, Florida.

Blackham, G. J., & Silberman, A. (1980). Modification of child and adolescent behavior (3rd ed.). Belmont, CA: Wadsworth.

Blackwood, R. (1970). The operant conditioning of verbally mediated self-control in the classroom. Journal of School Psychology, 8, 251-258.

Blanchard, K., & Johnson, S. (1982). The one minute manager. New York: William Morrow and Company, Inc.

Bolstad, O., & Johnson, S. (1972). Self-regulation in the modification of disruptive classroom behavior. Journal of Applied Behavior Analysis, 5, 443-454.

Borstein, P., & Quevillon, R. (1976). The effects of a self-instructional package on overactive preschool boys. Journal of Applied Behavior Analysis, 9, 179-188.

Broden, M., Bruce, C., Mitchell, M., Carter, V., & Hall, R. V. (1970). Effects of teacher attention on attending behavior of two boys at adjacent desks. Journal of Applied Behavior Analysis, 3, 205-211.

Brophy, J. E. (1983). Classroom organization and management. The Elementary School Journal, 83(1), 265-285.

Brown, L., Bellamy, R., Perlmutter, L., Sackowitz, P., & Sontag, E. (1972). The development of quality, quantity and durability in the work performance of retarded students in a public school prevocational workshop. Training School Bulletin, 69, 58-69.

Brown, L., Johnson, S., Gadberry, E., & Fenrick, N. (1971). Increasing individual and assembly line production rates of retarded students. Training School Bulletin, 67, 206-213.

Camp, B., & Bash, M. (1978). Think aloud: Group manual. (Rev. ed.). Denver: University of Colorado Medical School.

Cloward, R. (1967). Studies in tutoring. Journal of Experimental Education, 36, 14-25.

Csapo, M. (1972). Peer models reverse the "one bad apple spoils the barrel" theory. Teaching Exceptional Children. 5, 20-24.

Darveaux, D. S. (1984). The good behavior game plus merit: Controlling disruptive behavior and improving student motivation. School Psychology Review, 13, 510-514.

Doyle, W. (1980). Classroom management. West Lafayette, Indiana: Kappa Delta Pi.

Drabman, R. S., Spitalnik, R., & O'Leary, K. D. (1973). Teaching self-control to disruptive children. Journal of Abnormal Psychology, 82, 10-16.

Eaton, M., & Hansen, C. (1978). Classroom organization and management. In N. Haring, T. Lovitt, M. Eaton, & C. Hansen (Eds.), The fourth R: Research in the classroom. Columbus, OH: Charles E. Merrill.

Evertson, C. M., Emmer, E. T., Clements, B. S., Sanford, J. P., Worsham, M. E. (1984). Classroom management for elementary teachers. Englewood Cliffs, NJ: Prentice-Hall, Inc.

Fabry, B. D., Mayhew, G. L. & Hanson, A. (1984). Incidental teaching of mentally retarded students within a token system. American Journal of Mental Deficiency, 89, 29-36.

Foxx, M. R. (1982). Decreasing behaviors: Of severely retarded and autistic persons. Champaign, Ill: Research Press.

Gallagher, P. A. (1979). Teaching students with behavior disorders: Techniques for classroom instruction. Denver, CO: Love.

Glasser, W. (1965). Reality therapy. New York: Harper & Row, Inc.

Glasser, W. (1978). Disorders in our schools: Causes and remedies. Phi Delta Kappa, 59(5), 332-333.

Glynn, E., Thomas, J., & Shee, S. (1973). Behavioral self-control of on-task behavior in an elementary school classroom. Journal of Applied Behavior Analysis, 6, 105-113.

Good, T. L., Brophy, J. E. (1978). Looking in classrooms. New York: Harper & Row, Inc.

Greenwood, C. R., Dinwiddie, G., Terry, B., Wade, L., Stanley, S. O., Thibadeau, S., & Delquadri, J. C. (1984). Teacher- versus peer-mediated instruction: An ecobehavioral analysis of achievement outcomes. Journal of Applied Behavior Analysis, 17, 521-538.

Harris, V. W., & Sherman, J. A. (1973). Use and analysis of the "good behavior game" to reduce disruptive classroom behavior. Journal of Applied Behavior Analysis, 6, 405-417.

Humphrey, L., & Karoly, P. (1978). Self-management in the classroom: Self-imposed response cost versus self-reward. Behavior Therapy, 9, 592-601.

Iwata, B. A., & Bailey, J. S. (1974). Reward versus cost token systems: An analysis of the effects on students and teachers. Journal of Applied Behavior Analysis, 7, 567-576.

Jason, L. A., & Rebeck, P. R. (1984). Reducing excessive television viewing. Child & Family Behavior Therapy, 6, 61-69.

Johnston, J. M., Pennypacker, H. S. (1980). Strategies and tactics of human behavioral research. Hillsdale, NJ: Lawrence Erlbaum Associates.

Kaufman, K., & O'Leary, K. (1972). Reward, cost, and self-evaluation procedures for disruptive adolescents in a psychiatric hospital school. Journal of Applied Behavior Analysis, 5, 293-309.

Lindsley, O. R. (1968). A reliable wrist counter for recording behavior rates. Journal of Applied Behavior Analysis, 1, 77.

Lindsley, O. R. (1980). Key note address. Precision Teaching Conference, Orlando, Florida

Lochman, J. E., Burch, P. R., Curry, J. F., & Lampron, L. B. (1984). Treatment and generalization effects of cognitive-behavioral and goal-setting interventions with aggressive boys. Journal of Consulting and Clinical Psychology, 52, 915-916.

Long, N. J., Newman, R. G. (1971). Managing surface behavior of children in schools. In N. J. Long, W. C. Morse, & R. G. Newman (Eds), Conflict in the classroom: The education of emotionally disturbed children (2nd ed.). Belmont, CA: Wadsworth.

Lovitt, T. C. (1973). Self-management projects with children with behavioral disabilities. Journal of Learning Disabilities, 6, 138-150.

Lovitt, T. C. (1984). Tactics for teaching. Columbus, OH: Charles E. Merrill

Luiselli, J., & Downing, J. (1980). Improving a student's arithmetic performance using feedback and reinforcement procedures. Education and Treatment of Children, 3, 45-49.

Lupin, M. (1977). Peace, harmony, awareness. Austin, TX: Learning Concepts.

Mahoney, M. J., & Thoresen, C. E. (1974). Self-control: Power to the person. Monterey, CA: Brooks-Cole.

Mercer, C. D., & Mercer, A. R. (1985). Teaching students with learning problems. Columbus, OH: Charles E. Merrill.

Mitchell, Z. P., & Milan, M. A. (1983). Imitation of high-interest comic strip models' appropriate classroom behavior: Acquisition and generalization. Child & Family Behavior Therapy, 5, (2), 15-30.

Moletzky, B. (1974). Behavior recording as treatment: A brief note. Behavior Therapy, 5, 107-111.

Murphy, L., & Ross, S. M. (1983). Student self-control as a basis for instructional adaptation with behaviorally disordered children. Behavioral Disorders, 8, (4), 237-243.

Nietupski, J., Stainback, W., Gleissner, L., Stainback, S., & Nietuski, S. H. (1983). Effects of socially outgoing versus withdrawn nonhandicapped peer partners on nonhandicapped/handicapped student interactions. Behavioral Disorders, 8, 244-250.

O'Leary, K. D., & O'Leary, S. G. (1972). Classroom management. New York: Pergamon Press.

Olson, Judy. (1982). Treatment perspectives. In B. Algozzine, Problem behavior management. Gaithersburg, MD: Aspen Systems Corp.

Orelove, F. (1982). Developing daily schedules for classrooms of severely handicapped students. Education and Treatment of Children, 5, 59-68.

Paine, S. C., Radicchi, J., Rosellini, L. C., Deutchman, L., & Darch, C. B. (1983). Structuring your classroom for academic success. Champaign, IL: Research Press Company.

Peterson, S. K. (1985). Cueing and reinforcing independent work habits. Special Education Today, II, (1) 7.

Peterson, S. K. (1985). Improving work completion by beating the clock. Special Education Today, II (2) 4-5.

Peterson, S. K. (1984). Self-report used to monitor and change positive and negative verbalizations. Journal of Precision Teaching, 5, 9-11.

Phillips, E. L. (1968). Achievement place: Token reinforcement procedures in a home-style rehabilitation setting for "pre-delinquent" boys. Journal of Applied Behavior Analysis, 1, 213-223.

Phillips, E. L., Phillips, E. A., Fixsen, D. L., & Wolf, M. M. (1971). Achievement place: Modification of the behaviors of pre-delinquent boys within a token economy. Journal of Applied Behavior Analysis, 4, 45-59.

Piersel, W., & Kratochwill, T. (1979). Self-observation and behavior change: Applications to academic and adjustment problems through behavioral consultation. Journal of School Psychology, 17, 151-161.

Rainwater, N., & Ayllon, R. (1976). Increasing academic performance by using a timer as an antecedent stimulus: A study of four cases. Behavior Therapy, 7, 672-677.

Rolider, A. and Van Houten, R. (1985). How to eliminate severe inappropriate behavior. Paper presented at the Florida Association for Behavior Analysis convention, Tampa, Florida

Rosenshine, B., Furst, N. (1973). The use of direct observation to study teaching. In R. M. W. Travers (Ed), Second handbook of research on teaching. Chicago: Rand McNally.

Schneider, R. A., & Dolnick, M. (1976). The turtle technique: An extended case study of self-control in the classroom. Psychology in the Schools, 13, 449-453.

Shafer, M. S., Egel, A. L., & Neef, N. A. (1984). Training mildly handicapped peers to facilitate changes in the social interaction skills of autistic children. Journal of Applied Behavior Analysis, 17, 461-476.

Solomon, R. W., & Wahler, R. G. (1973). Peer reinforcement control of classroom problem behavior. Journal of Applied Behavior Analysis, 6, 49-56.

Stephens, T. M. (1977). Teaching skills to children with learning and behavior disorders. Columbus, OH: Charles E. Merrill.

Tenenbaum, H. A. and Wolking, W. D. (1981). Academic athletes. Behavioral Education, 2, (2).

Thoreson, C. E., & Mahoney, M. J. (1974). Behavioral self-control. New York: Holt, Rinehart, & Winston.

Wilson, J. (1978). Selecting educational materials and resources. In D. D. Hammill, & N. R. Bartel (Eds), Teaching children with learning and behavior problems (2nd ed.). Boston: Allyn & Bacon.

Winkler, R. C. (1970). Management of chronic psychiatric patients by a token reinforcement system. Journal of Applied Behavior Analysis, 3, 47-55.

Wolf, M. M., Hanley, E. L., King, L. A., Lachowicz, J., & Giles, D. K. (1970). The timer-game: A variable interval contingency for the management of out-of-seat behavior. Exceptional Children, 37, 113-117.

Wolfgang, C. H., & Glickman, C. D. (1980). Solving discipline problems. Boston, MA: Allyn and Bacon.

Workman, E. A. (1982). Teaching behavioral self-control to students. Texas: PRO-ED.

Workman, E. & Hector, M. (1978). Behavior self control in classroom settings: A review of the literature. Journal of School Psychology, 16, 227-236.

Zimmerman, J., Stuckey, T. E., Garlick, B. J., & Miller, M. (1969). Effects of token reinforcement on productivity in multiply-handicapped clients in a sheltered workshop. Rehabilitation Literature, 30, 34-41.

Behavior – Technique Matrix

BEHAVIOR CLASSES

TECHNIQUES	Academic Improvement	Affective	Aggression	Compliance
Beat the Clock				X
Behavioral Self-Control	X	X	X	X
Cognitive Modeling	X	X	X	X
Contracting	X	X	X	X
The Good Behavior Game		X	X	X
Independent Work Chart				X
Modeling		X	X	X
Peer Tutoring	X	X		
Reality Therapy		X		
Response Cost System		X	X	X
Systematic Desensitization		X		
The Timer Game		X		X
Token Reinforcement System	X	X	X	X
The Turtle Technique			X	

ABOUT THE AUTHORS

Susan K. Peterson is an associate instructor at the University of Florida. She is currently the project manager for the Multidisciplinary Diagnostic and Training Program. Susan has a variety of teaching experiences including employability skills to economically disadvantaged adults, social studies and compensatory math to high school students, and basic skills to elementary school students with learning, emotional, and/or medical problems. Susan received her B. S. in Sociology from Florida Southern College, her M.Ed. in Special Education from the University of Florida, and is currently finishing the requirements for her Ph.D. in Special Education with a minor in Educational Administration.

Henry Tenenbaum is principal at Volusia Avenue School for emotionally handicapped students in Daytona Beach, Florida. Previously he was the school psychologist for the Multidisciplinary Diagnostic and Training Program at the University of Florida. Henry's specialization areas include direct assessment, applied behavior analysis, microcomputing, and management of students with severe behavioral disorders. Henry received his B. A. in Experimental Psychology from Florida Atlantic University, his Ed.S. in School Psychology from Florida International University and his Ph.D. in School Psychology from the University of Florida.